SCRIPTURES FOR
Living Free

SCRIPTURES FOR
Living Free

PREPARED BY
NEVA COYLE

BETHANY HOUSE PUBLISHERS
MINNEAPOLIS, MINNESOTA 55438
A Division of Bethany Fellowship, Inc.

Scriptures for Living Free
Neva Coyle

ISBN 0-87123-576-5
Copyright © 1982
Neva Coyle
All Rights Reserved

Published by Bethany House Publishers
A Division of Bethany Fellowship, Inc.
6820 Auto Club Road, Minneapolis, Minnesota 55438

Printed in the United States of America

Publisher's Note

The Scripture quotations are taken from The Amplified Bible, and condensed to fit the unique format of the book. The section divisions and scriptures correspond with those in *Daily Thoughts on Living Free*, by Neva Coyle. Flip the pages consecutively to the end and then turn the book around and continue.

After reading the devotional and scripture for the day in *Daily Thoughts on Living Free*, you may conveniently display the corresponding scripture on your dresser or countertop as a reminder for meditation or memorization throughout the day or week.

Roman Reinforcements

The book of Romans is a book of reinforcement. You can refer to these mighty words and phrases whenever you need help, when you feel that you have "fired your last bullet." When certain defeat or failure are at hand, you can be reinforced with the Word of God.

As you read, remember that you are placing within your spirit the very reinforcement that you will need to go through the day victoriously.

He who dwells in the secret place
of the Most High shall remain
stable and fixed under the
shadow of the Almighty.
Psalm 91:1

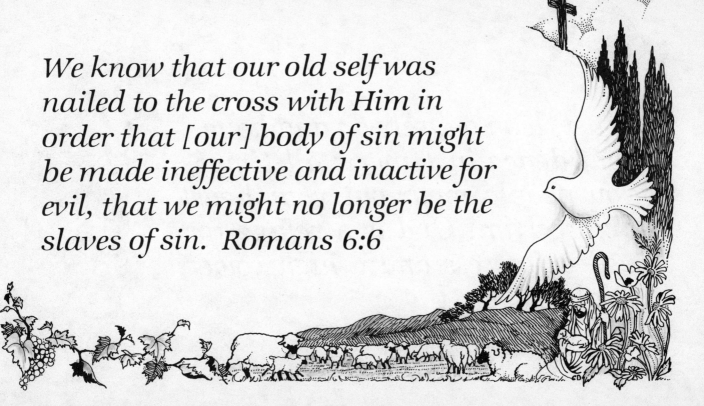

We know that our old self was nailed to the cross with Him in order that [our] body of sin might be made ineffective and inactive for evil, that we might no longer be the slaves of sin. Romans 6:6

Trust, lean on, rely on and have confidence in Him at all times, you people; pour out your heart before Him. God is a refuge for us—a fortress and a high tower.
Psalm 62:8

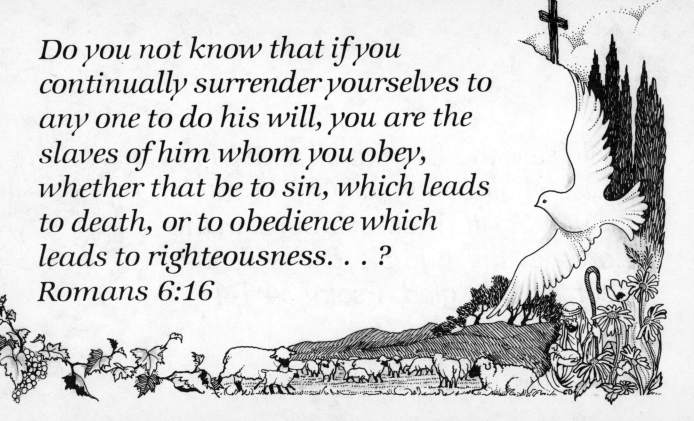

Do you not know that if you continually surrender yourselves to any one to do his will, you are the slaves of him whom you obey, whether that be to sin, which leads to death, or to obedience which leads to righteousness. . . ?
Romans 6:16

I will bless the Lord at all times; His praise shall continually be in my mouth. My life makes its boast in the Lord; let the humble and afflicted hear and be glad. Psalm 34:1-4

But now since you have been set free from sin and have become the slaves of God, you have your present reward in holiness and its end is eternal life. Romans 6:22

The Lord is my light and my salvation; whom shall I fear or dread? The Lord is the refuge and stronghold of my life; of whom shall I be afraid? Wait and hope for and expect the Lord; be brave and of good courage. Psalm 27:1, 14

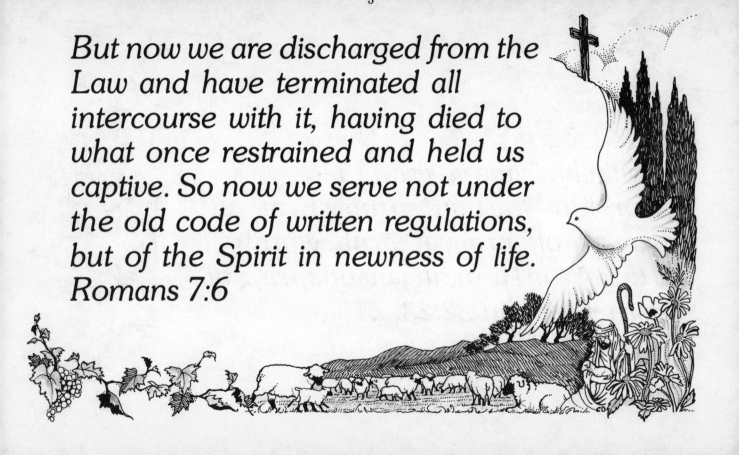

But now we are discharged from the Law and have terminated all intercourse with it, having died to what once restrained and held us captive. So now we serve not under the old code of written regulations, but of the Spirit in newness of life.
Romans 7:6

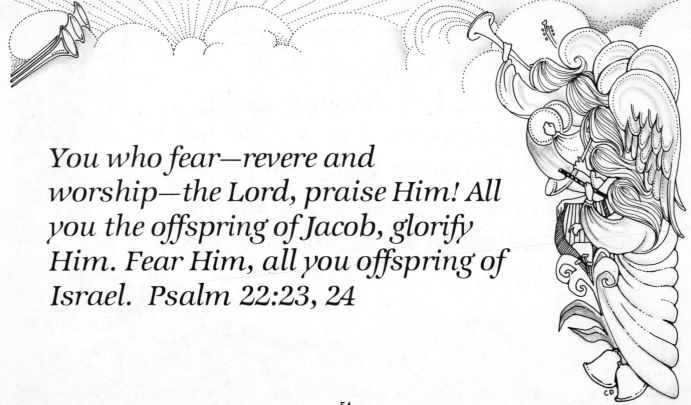

You who fear—revere and worship—the Lord, praise Him! All you the offspring of Jacob, glorify Him. Fear Him, all you offspring of Israel. Psalm 22:23, 24

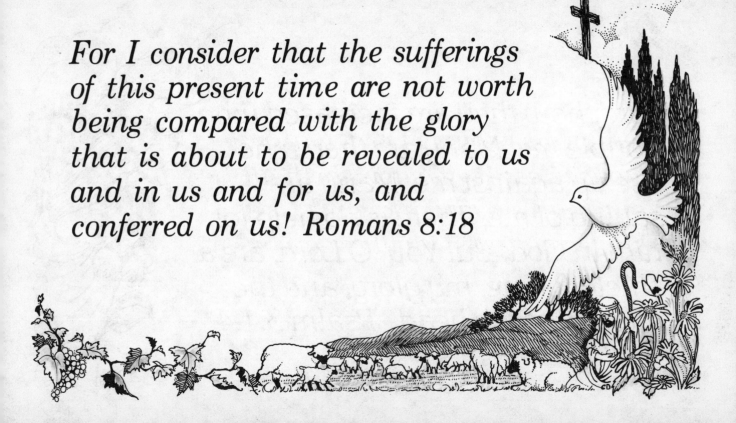

For I consider that the sufferings of this present time are not worth being compared with the glory that is about to be revealed to us and in us and for us, and conferred on us! Romans 8:18

Lord, how they are increased who trouble me! Many are they who rise up against me. Many are saying of me, There is no help for him in God. But You, O Lord, are a shield for me, my glory, and the lifter up of my head. Psalm 3:1-4

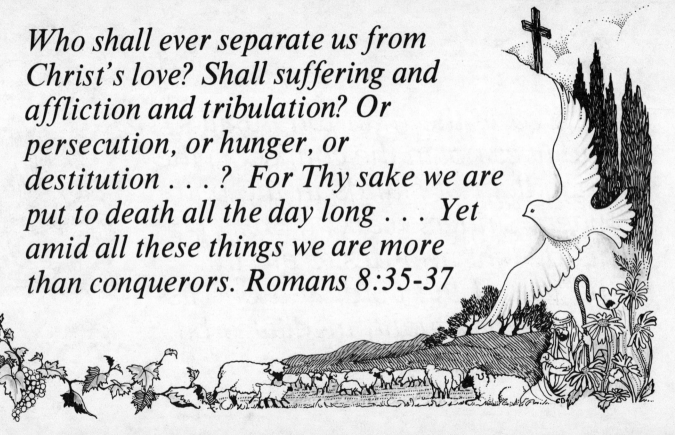

Who shall ever separate us from Christ's love? Shall suffering and affliction and tribulation? Or persecution, or hunger, or destitution . . . ? For Thy sake we are put to death all the day long . . . Yet amid all these things we are more than conquerors. Romans 8:35-37

Blessed is the man who walks and lives not in the counsel of the ungodly, nor stands in the path where sinners walk... But his delight and desire are in the law of the Lord, and on His law he habitually meditates by day and by night. Psalm 1:1, 2

51

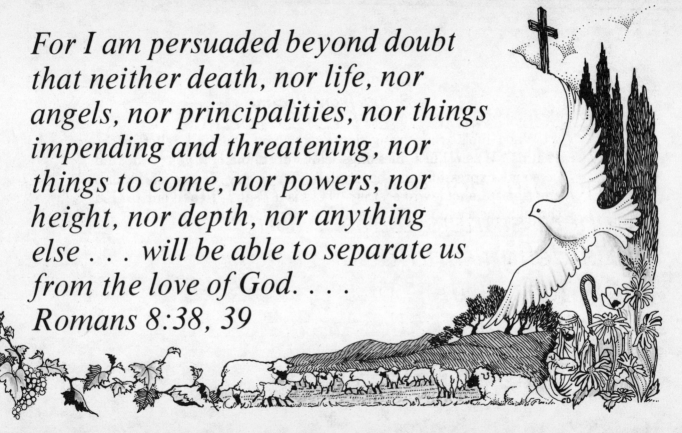

*For I am persuaded beyond doubt
that neither death, nor life, nor
angels, nor principalities, nor things
impending and threatening, nor
things to come, nor powers, nor
height, nor depth, nor anything
else . . . will be able to separate us
from the love of God. . . .*
Romans 8:38, 39

Songs from Psalms

When life's trials bring depression, you can find relief in the Psalms. When life's blessings call for rejoicing, you can find personal expression in the Psalms. For every degree of human emotion from agony to ecstasy, there is a Psalm. Reach out to God through the Psalms; His promise is that He will be found.

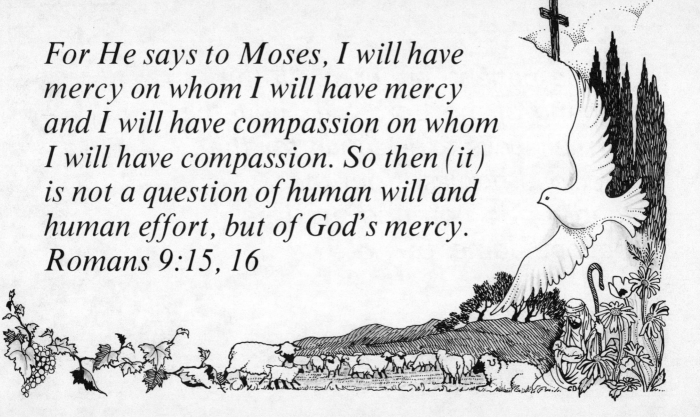

For He says to Moses, I will have mercy on whom I will have mercy and I will have compassion on whom I will have compassion. So then (it) is not a question of human will and human effort, but of God's mercy. Romans 9:15, 16

So be patient, brethren, till the coming of the Lord. See how the farmer waits expectantly for the precious harvest from the land. . . . So you also must be patient. James 5:7, 8

Ephesians Encouragements

The book of Ephesians contains wonderful encouragement. The Word of God is mighty, and it was written for you. No matter how you feel right now, God's Word remains the same. It is the only truth you can actually count on.

To face the hard situations of life, to be strong enough to confront any circumstance in a positive manner, we must first be in the habit of praising and blessing God. Won't you stop today and give praise to God, blessing the name of the Lord?

But He gives us more and more grace. That is why He says, God sets Himself against the proud and haughty, but gives grace to the lowly—those who are humble-minded. *James 4:6*

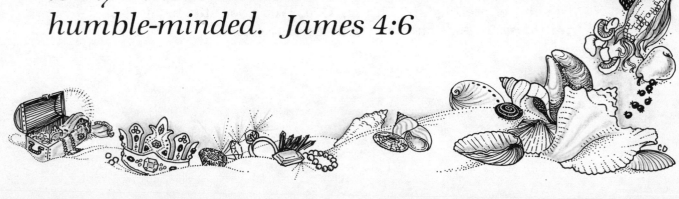

Even as He chose us—actually picked us out for Himself as His own—in Christ before the foundation of the world; that we should be holy and blameless in His sight, even above reproach, before Him in love. Ephesians 1:4

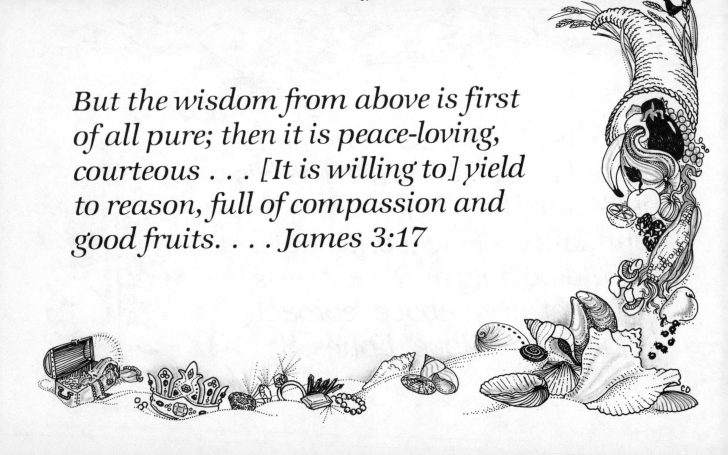

But the wisdom from above is first of all pure; then it is peace-loving, courteous . . . [It is willing to] yield to reason, full of compassion and good fruits. . . . James 3:17

In Him we have redemption through His blood, the remission of our offenses in accordance with the riches and the generosity of His gracious favor, which He lavished upon us in every kind of wisdom and understanding. Ephesians 1:7, 8

13

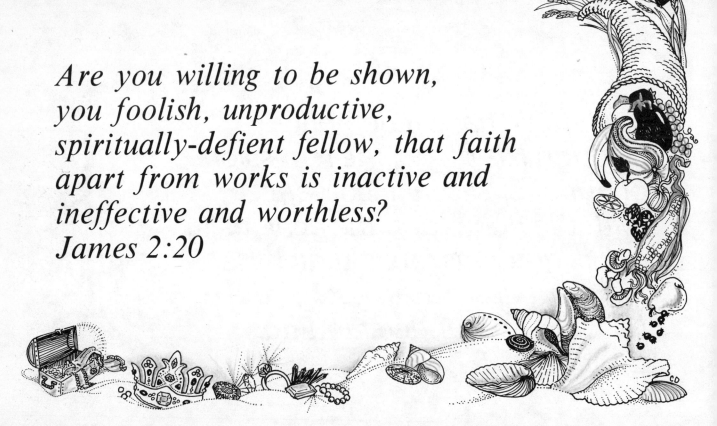

Are you willing to be shown,
you foolish, unproductive,
spiritually-defient fellow, that faith
apart from works is inactive and
ineffective and worthless?
James 2:20

Even when we were dead by shortcomings and trespasses, He made us alive together in fellowship and in union with Christ—He gave us the very life of Christ Himself, the same new life with which He quickened Him. . . . Ephesians 2:5

Obey the message; be doers of the Word, and not merely listeners to it, betraying yourselves. James 1:22

For we are God's handiwork, recreated in Christ Jesus, that we may do those good works which God predestined for us, that we should walk in them—living the good life which He prearranged and made ready for us to live.
Ephesians 2:10

Blessed, happy, to be envied is the man who is patient under trial and stands up under temptation, for when he has stood the test and been approved he will receive (the) crown of life which God has promised to those who love Him. James 1:12

Therefore you are no longer outsiders—exiles, migrants and aliens, excluded from the rights of citizens; but you now share citizenship with the saints—God's own people, consecrated and set apart for Himself; and you belong to God's household. Ephesians 2:19

If any of you is deficient in wisdom, let him ask of the giving God [who gives] to every one liberally and ungrudgingly, without reproaching or faultfinding, and it will be given him. James 1:5

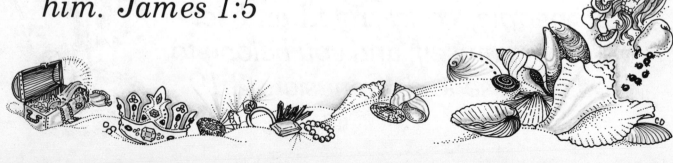

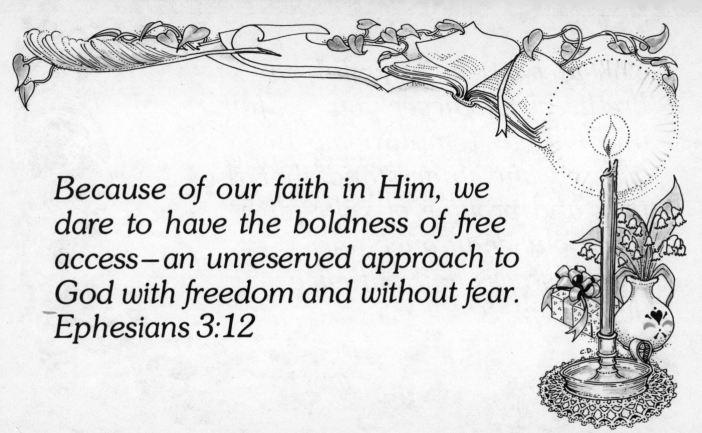

Because of our faith in Him, we dare to have the boldness of free access—an unreserved approach to God with freedom and without fear. Ephesians 3:12

Consider it wholly joyful, my brethren, whenever you . . . fall into various temptations. Be assured and understand that the trial and proving of your faith bring out endurance and steadfastness and patience.
James 1:2, 3

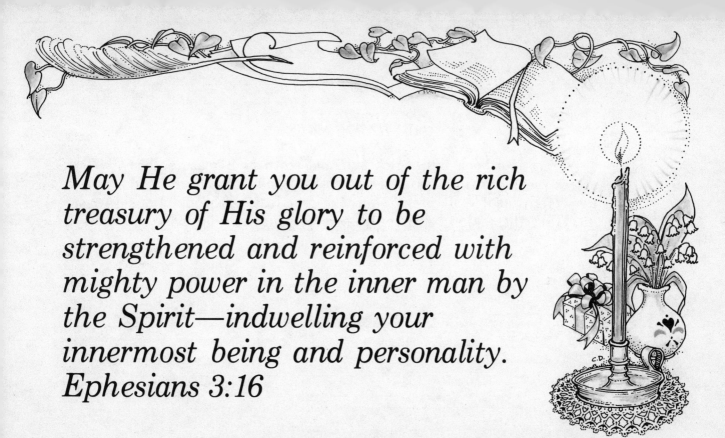

*May He grant you out of the rich treasury of His glory to be strengthened and reinforced with mighty power in the inner man by the Spirit—indwelling your innermost being and personality.
Ephesians 3:16*

Gems from James

James is a book full of rich spiritual truth and treasure. The verses speak of principles, and the work of God in the hearts and lives of His people. James gives us the practicals of the victorious life. Take these verses and apply them to your everyday life.

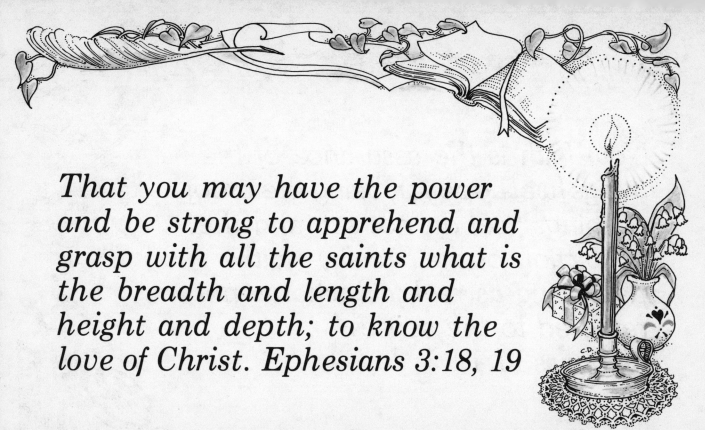

*That you may have the power
and be strong to apprehend and
grasp with all the saints what is
the breadth and length and
height and depth; to know the
love of Christ. Ephesians 3:18, 19*

Now faith is the assurance of the things [we] hope for, being the proof of things [we] do not see and the conviction of their reality—faith perceiving as real fact what is not revealed to the senses.

Hebrews 11:1

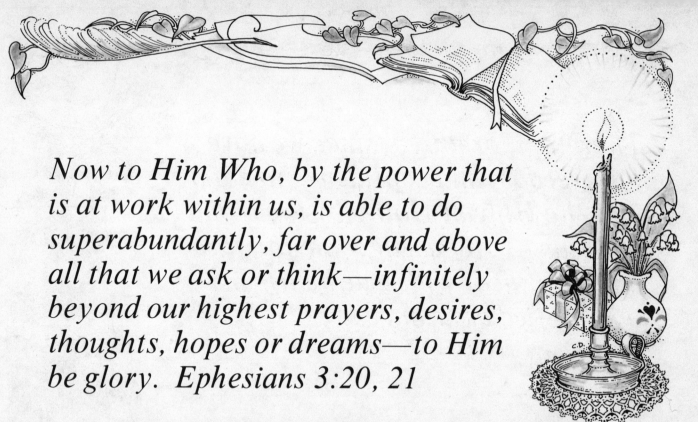

Now to Him Who, by the power that is at work within us, is able to do superabundantly, far over and above all that we ask or think—infinitely beyond our highest prayers, desires, thoughts, hopes or dreams—to Him be glory. Ephesians 3:20, 21

Therefore, brethren, since we have full freedom and confidence to enter into the Holy of Holies by the blood of Jesus . . . let us all come forward and draw near with true hearts in unqualified assurance.
Hebrews 10:19-22

Philippian Friends

Dig now into Philippians with me, and discover the friendliness of the Truth. Apply it to your life. Stop telling yourself you can't make it when the truth is that you can. Don't say that God has given up on you. Philippians says that He began a good work, that it is a good work and that He won't quit. Don't say you don't have any friends; you have these "Philippians Friends," and you have Jesus.

Furthermore, every priest stands ministering daily, offering the same sacrifices over and over again, which never are able to strip the sins, and take them away. Hebrews 10:11

And I am convinced and sure of this very thing, that He Who began a good work in you will continue until the day of Jesus Christ—right up to the time of His return—developing and perfecting and bringing it to full completion in you. Philippians 1:6

Under the Law almost everything is purified by means of blood, and without the shedding of blood there is neither release from sin and its guilt nor the remission of the due and merited punishment for sins.
Hebrews 9:22

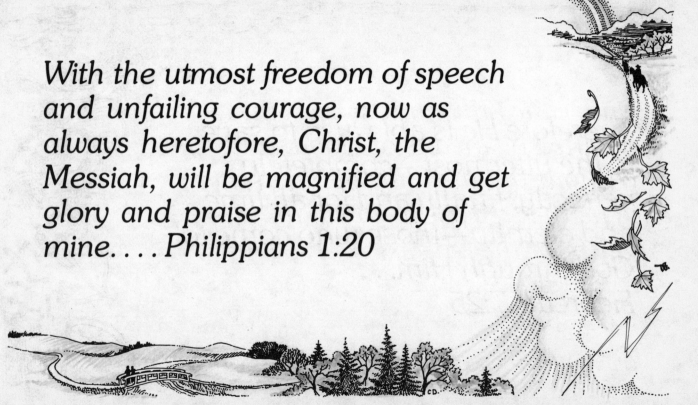

With the utmost freedom of speech and unfailing courage, now as always heretofore, Christ, the Messiah, will be magnified and get glory and praise in this body of mine.... Philippians 1:20

Therefore He is able also to save to the uttermost—completely, perfectly, finally and for all time and eternity—those who come to God through Him. . . .
Hebrews 7:25

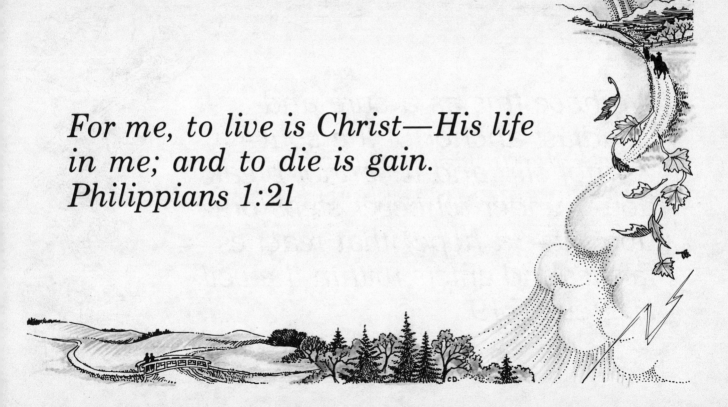

24

For me, to live is Christ—His life in me; and to die is gain.
Philippians 1:21

We have this as a sure and steadfast anchor of the soul—it cannot slip and it cannot break down under whoever steps out upon it—(a hope) that reaches farther and enters within the veil.
Hebrews 6:19

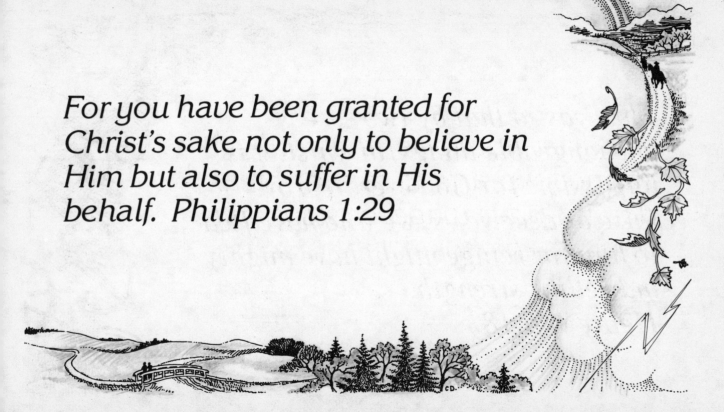

25

For you have been granted for Christ's sake not only to believe in Him but also to suffer in His behalf. Philippians 1:29

This was so that by two unchangeable things, in which it is impossible for God ever to prove false or deceive us, we who have fled to him for refuge might have mighty indwelling strength. . . .
Hebrews 6:18

34

That I may know Him—that I may progressively become more deeply and intimately acquainted with Him . . . And that I may in that same way come to know the power outflowing from His resurrection. Philippians 3:10

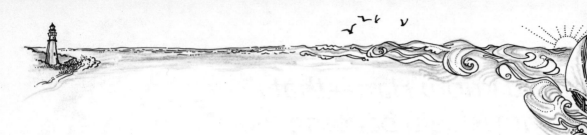

*God also, in His desire to show
more convincingly and beyond
doubt, to those who want to inherit
the promise, the unchangeableness
of His purpose and plan, intervened
with an oath. Hebrews 6:17*

27

One thing I do—it is my one aspiration: forgetting what lies behind and straining forward to what lies ahead, I press on toward the goal to win the prize to which God in Christ Jesus is calling us upward. Philippians 3:13, 14

But we do desire for each of you to show the same diligence and sincerity . . . behaving as do those who through faith, and by practice of patient endurance and waiting are inheriting the promises.
Hebrews 6:11, 12

28

Rejoice in the Lord always— delight, gladden yourselves in Him; again I say, Rejoice! Let all men know and perceive and recognize your unselfishness—your considerateness, your forbearing spirit. Philippians 4:4, 5

Hope from Hebrews

Have you ever felt as though you couldn't see the end of the tunnel? Have you felt that all the miracles happen to everyone else? You need hope—and it is promised to you. It is a gift from God. If you don't feel hopeful now, you will. When your hope is founded in Him, based on His Word, the Father will allow you the wonderful peace that accompanies such a hope.

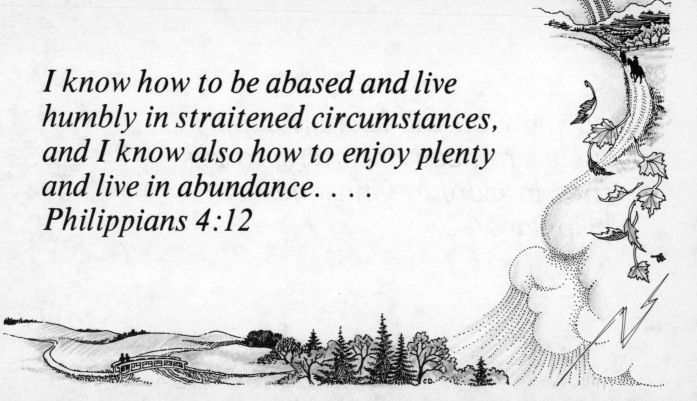

I know how to be abased and live humbly in straitened circumstances, and I know also how to enjoy plenty and live in abundance. . . .
Philippians 4:12

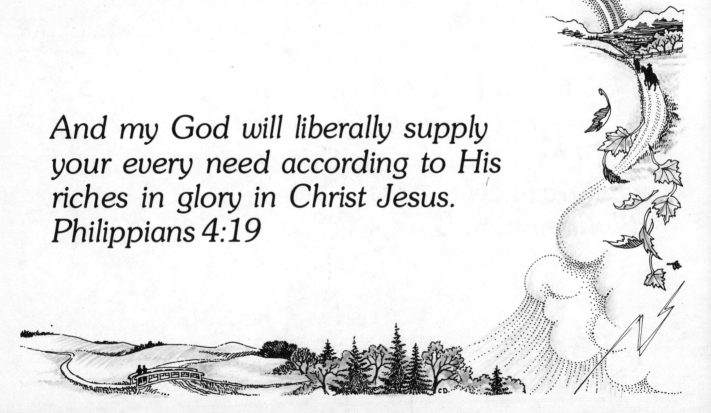

And my God will liberally supply your every need according to His riches in glory in Christ Jesus. Philippians 4:19